A to Z of Inspiring Early Years: Paragraphs

A to Z of Inspiring Early Years: Paragraphs

by Laura Henry

Dip In and Dip Out books
C/O Childcare Consultancy
Acorn House
74 – 94 Cherry Orchard Road
Croydon
CR0 6BA

www.dipinanddipoutbooks.com

www.childcareconsult.co.uk

© Dip In and Dip Out Books

ISBN-13: 978-1492859123
ISBN-10: 1492859125

About the Author:

Laura Henry is a childcare specialist who has spent most of her working life either working directly with children or supporting others who work with children.

She currently delivers bespoke training sessions and unique consultancy support. Laura is passionate about children and their families, writing extensively for Early Years journals, and is often called upon to share her specialist knowledge on Early Years issues internationally.

She is also the mother of two teenage sons.

Please feel free to contact her:
laura@childcareconsult.co.uk

Follow her on Twitter: @LauraChildcare

"If I can inspire one educator through my work, imagine how many children they will go on to inspire."

--Laura Henry, 2012

Introduction

When training or working face-to-face with educators they often say to me, "Laura, what you said was truly inspiring". I reply that I ought to write it down and use it within an article or a blog! I don't usually remember precisely what I have said, as when I speak about Early Years it comes from the heart.

This was how the idea for this book of inspiring paragraphs came about. By sharing with Early Years colleagues, I truly hope to have a positive impact on their work with children.

Although the book is laid out alphabetically, please feel free to pick and choose paragraphs as you see fit. You could reflect on a letter each day, once a week or once a month or use it within staff meetings to suggest potential improvements to your practice.

You could brainstorm ideas per letter; jot down ideas in a reflective note book, or create an inspirational display. Look for images that reflect the letters to enhance your displays.

Please feel free to contact me and share how these inspirational paragraphs have positively impacted on you as an educator, your setting and the children and families with whom you work.

For your reference I have clarified a few key terms at the beginning and included helpful appendices at the end.

Key Terms:

Early Years Educator: Practitioner, nursery nurse, childminder, teacher, assistant, play worker, nanny

Parent: Carer or any other significant adult

Setting: Nursery, pre-school, kindergarten, school, home-based, out-of-school care, crèche

Key Person: The person who has the primary responsibility for the child on a day-to-day basis

Always

What is your 'always' within your day-to-day practice? This is something that you always do in your practice that has a positive and lasting impact on children. Your 'always' could be linked to your practice, for example 'always' making a special effort to connect with and say hello to parents, 'always' having a special moment for a meaningful conversation with a child. When you learn something new about a child, how do you 'always' use the information to have an impact on your practice?

Boomerang

We are fortunate within Early Years to receive a number of gems from other educators, parents and even the children we work with. It could be a book that has had a particular impact upon our practice, a special resource or a gem from a colleague or parent. How do you boomerang this gem back to the person or share the gem with others? Think of this like a ripple effect of sharing: it could be that you mention the name of the gem, share the gem with others or give back the gem to the person. Keep the 'boomerang' in the air so it goes backwards and forwards to each other, keeping the positivity of the gem alive.

Community

The community has a real relevance within our day-to-day work with children and families. It is useful to remember the African proverb: **"It takes a village to raise a child".** How do you engage with the local community? Do you take children out on regular walks within their community so that they feel a sense of belonging and connect to their community? Do you point out key locations, shops, places of interests, and parks or recreation grounds or areas of natural beauty? Who are your key community people within the community:

faith leaders, police officers, fire officers, shop keepers? Taking children out on a regular basis helps them to create a real sense of connection with and belonging to their community. Think about creating a scrap book of visits to the community with a map of the different places that the children connected with.

Developing

You should be developing your practice continuously. Which areas are you currently developing? How will these changes impact upon your practice? An example would be growing a particular area, such as outdoor learning. Alternatively you could focus on developing your knowledge of child protection or special needs. It is important to create clear goals - use the SMART acronym: S-Specific, M-Measurable, A-Attainable, R-Realistic, T-Timely **(Appendix 1).** By using SMART goals you are more likely to make real progress and so achieve your goals. As a really well tried and effective method, SMART goals help you to clarify what you are developing and so lead to an improved practice. It is crucial to share what you are developing with your colleagues and likewise that they share what they are developing with you. This way you will have a real impact on your practice.

Elevating

Aim high! I strongly believe that children deserve the best; we should continually be elevating our practice. To me, elevating is linking to the standards that we set, creating a culture of aiming high for the children we work with and not settling for second best. Children deserve to be in an environment where adults always aim high, thus elevating the practice.

Family

The child and family are part of your setting. It is important to recognise that it is not only the parents we include within the family unit but also step-parents, aunts, uncle, siblings, grandparents and any other significant family members or friends whom the child regards as family. Do you know who the child lives with and where? How many siblings do they have? Is there a blended approach to the child's home care, for example does the child live part of the week with one parent, and the other part with another parent or grandparents? How do you discuss this with the child and the family? How do you celebrate and embrace the child and their family in your day-to-day practice?

Gazing

We need to make sure that we take time within our busy day to stop, look and listen: reflect deeply on what each child is doing. What is the child really doing within those activities and experiences? What is having an impact on the child's behaviour? Can you take time out to gaze from the child's perspective? What does the child see? How does the child see the adults who teach and care for them? Only when we take time to gaze can we truly reflect, assess and plan for each child's ongoing learning, providing the most appropriate support for each child's development.

Holistic

Bringing together holistically, theoretical and philosophical approaches and practices into your day to day work is very important. Firstly, do you know what approaches and practices there are and what they mean? For example, Montessori (Find and Return), High Scope (Plan, Do and Review) and Reggio Emilia (Children being the leaders in their learning.) There are many others. If you are not aware of these, it might be useful to research what they are and what they mean. Educators with a solid understanding take what could be called a 'pick 'n' mix' approach, adopting one or more of the theoretical and philosophical practices that mirror their values. However, to understand theoretical and philosophical practices, one must have a thorough understanding of child development. This means having an awareness of the ages, stages and abilities of how a child learns and develops.

Inspiring

In my career I have been inspired by many people:-ranging from my grandmother's positive attitude and my mother's words of wisdom, to books I have read, or inspirational speeches from Early Years experts, or from the words of a child, parent or colleague. One thing I am sure of is that I continue to be inspired by so many people; this has had a massive impact on my career, enabling me to share with others. What has inspired you in your career? How has it made a difference to your practice? How has it changed what you do with children on a day-to-day basis?

Jump and

Pump™

Working with children for up to twelve hours a day can be tiring. I find that the afternoon can sometimes be a 'flat' period for both educators and children. What I mean by 'flat' is when I observe the time children are waking up from their sleep or staff returning from their lunch breaks and it's before afternoon tea. Normally this is between 2:00pm and 3:00pm. The energy levels are low, everyone is feeling lethargic and there is a shift in moods and feelings. What I recommend is 'jump and pump' which is a mini exercise or dance session. This could either be staff and children signing rhymes or songs or the use of recorded music. **(Appendix 2).** Anything that gets the body moving will help to revitalise both staff and children. You can set the length of time you do this based on the age, stage and ability of the children. This will give everyone enough 'fuel' for the rest of the day, promoting a healthy mind, body and spirit for children and staff alike.

Keep

There are times when, despite what is going on internally and externally, we need to keep going. There are constant changes in legislation and guidance, as well as changes that happen within our provision. Sometimes we have to implement changes that we'd rather resist, as we may feel they are not appropriate. However, we must remember to keep children at the forefront and keep their needs central to any changes.

Learning

How you learn and how you develop will have a profound impact on how the children in your practice learn and develop. It is important to take personal responsibility for your own Continuous Personal and Professional Development (CPPD). There are many ways to keep your skills and knowledge up-to-date; from attending face-to-face training, observing another colleague, having a mentor or coach, contributing to staff meetings, visiting other settings, reading journals and research (this includes making good use of the internet, especially reading and having an understanding of international Early Years issues). It may be helpful to have your own learning journal that includes your recent training, your reflections on that training, how you will change your practice as a consequence of the training and how you will share this with your colleagues. It is helpful to reflect upon your CPPD regularly **(Appendix 3),** thinking about the points above and how it has made a difference to your practice and to the outcomes for children.

Moments

There are numerous special 'moments' when we watch children. Observing the joy on a child's face when walking for the first time, children creating and directing their learning or a child carefully holding an insect in its hand. How do we capture and hold on to these moments within our own memory banks? Do we share these moments with children, parents and colleagues? We can use oral stories, we can take photographs, use videos or write about the moment. If we share these moments, we are then able to keep the momentum going, so that the sharing of these moments is repeated and becomes the norm within our day-to-day practice.

Noise

I am sure there are a lot of amazing things about your practice. However, there are times when we must create a bit of 'noise' about aspects of our practice that need to be improved. I would summarise this as: 'Disturb practice that needs disturbing and praise practice that needs praising'. It could be something to do with your own practice or the practice within your setting that you know and feel is not in the best interests of the children's welfare, development or learning. You might need to reflect on it, before sharing the 'noise' with a colleague or your line manager.

Make sure you can back up why the practice or thing needs disturbing, by linking to your setting's values, to legislation, guidance or good practice.

Open

How open are you to new ideas? What do you open up to on a daily or weekly basis? This could be opening up to an idea that a colleague has shared with you. Do you dismiss the idea? Do you explore the idea? Do you think how the idea could link to your practice and how this might impact on children's growth overall?

Person

Every child we work with is an exceptional person in their own right. How do we tailor our practice to their uniqueness? How do we give every child the right to be heard as stated within the United Nations Convention on the Rights of the Child? **(Appendix 4)** How do you personalise your practice to every child, so that they feel a sense of unity within your setting? Also think about those children with additional needs or disabilities, embrace the children's culture, race and religion. To have a personalised approach is all about knowing the children you work with directly; **(Appendix 5)** focusing on what they like doing, who the key people are in their lives and how you build rapport with children so they feel emotionally safe in your care. Reflect on the day-to-day activities that you provide for children: are they personalised to the each child's development and learning needs?

Quality

Quality is a word that means different things to different people. How do we clearly define what quality is? Quality should be linked to your values and ethos. I strongly believe that quality is about having high standards and principles that everyone in your setting maintains at all times.

Visualise your principles as a barrier, with the height of the barrier being determined by your standards of quality. Dropping your standards means compromising your principles. Continuing with this metaphor, if we think of the children's care, welfare and early learning as some of our principles, then poor quality will directly and adversely impact upon the children's care, welfare and early learning. **(Appendix 6).** There are a number of quality auditing schemes on the market or your setting may have its own. Settings that conduct regular audits, acknowledging what they do well in and what they need to improve upon, are more likely to maintain and improve on quality. Educators should also contribute to the auditing.

Relationships

When working with children and their families it is very important to foster positive and personal relationships. We need to reflect upon what we mean by the term 'relationship' within Early Years and what this looks like in practise, building on what we already know about the child and family. How we interact with children affects how they learn and develop. Remember the ground-breaking work of John Bowlby regarding attachments and how this links to the role of the Key Person with whom the child interacts every day. Do we have 'snuggle in times' with children and give 'Professional Love,' a term that Dr. Jools Page cites within her work? **(Appendix 7)**

Scrumptious

Food plays an important part within any Early Years setting; even if you are only providing sessional care, children will still be offered snacks. We have had so much information on healthy eating for children; many settings now embrace healthy eating by providing a range of nutritious snacks and meals. We should consider how we present food to children and how we celebrate meal times as a significant daily event within our setting. We should also consider how learning opportunities are naturally created within mealtimes: children helping to set the table, using maths to add up how many knives and forks are needed, finding out about the food, such as where it comes from and how it is made, grown and cooked (geography and science) and how we foster conversations and sharing at meal times (examples of personal, social and emotional development).

Teaching

There is a general misconception that teaching is only done when an educator stands at the front and teaches a group of children. This is wrong. Teaching is everything we do with young children, from showing and supporting a child how to put their shoes on, to reading a story or discussing personal safety. We should view teaching as the activities and experiences that we do with and for children throughout the whole day.

Universe

We can become very insular, focusing on our own setting and its development. While such development is important, we should consider having an awareness of other practices within our local community, further afield and internationally. Some settings have "twinned" with settings in another country, sharing ideas, their country's Early Years curriculum and teaching practices. It is also great for children to see children in other parts of their own country as well as overseas. This impacts on children positively. Using Skype or Face Time could be good for this.

Values

Every setting should have its own values and ethos. As a starting point, staff should reflect on their personal values and how these link to the setting's values. 'Values' are those things to which we attach importance, including the children, parents, environment and each other as a staff team. For example, what is important to you and what is important to your setting? This could start from your own value that children have a voice.

Wow

As adults there are many things that we see and embrace that make us stop and look a second time. These could be an artefact, a picture or a display in a shop. We may think, 'How did they do that?' or 'I wonder how that works?' or 'I so want to touch that object'. With this in mind, what do you bring into your setting that gives children the same wow feeling? Thinking about this from a sensory perspective, **(Appendix 8)** what do you have in the setting to give children the 'wow' feeling and a sense of wonder and awe? Will they investigate, find out more,

stimulate thoughts and conversations?
As an educator you should see it as your
personal responsibility to find things that
give children the 'wow' feeling. The 'wow'
doesn't have to cost money!

Xenodochical

Xenodochical comes from the Greek word and means how hospitable we are to others who we come into contact with within our setting. Thinking about this, how do you welcome visitors into your setting? How do you give a friendly smile to a parent visiting for the first time for a show around? How do you greet the child and their parent first thing in the morning? How do you connect with students and volunteers? How emotionally safe and welcoming is your environment? Do visitors leave your setting feeling that you have made a positive impact on them?

You

There is only one of you! As an individual you have so much to offer. Make a list of your skills, talents, expertise and knowledge. These might not have been gained solely within Early Years, but could be something that you have done outside work, perhaps as an interest or a hobby. How do you use your personal DNA within your setting to share with children, parents and colleagues to support your setting's continuous development?

Zeal

Make sure you remain enthusiastic, with
fire in your belly and a 'can do' approach.
Make sure your zeal rubs off onto your
colleagues and keeps everyone up-beat.
Let the oozing of your zeal drip onto the
setting.

Finally...

"Don't let what you can't do interfere with what you can do."

--John Wooden

Appendix

Appendix 1

Overview of 'SMART'

SMART stands for:

- **Specific**
- **Measurable**
- **Attainable**
- **Realistic**
- **Timely**

1 Specific

You are more likely to achieve a specific goal rather than a general goal. It is helpful to remember the six 'w' questions.

Who: who else is involved

What: what do you want to accomplish

Where: identify if there is a location in your setting

When: make sure you have a time frame

Which: identify if there are any constraints and/or requirements

Why: what will the benefit of achieving the goal

2 Measureable

How you set the criteria to measure how you progress towards completing every goal. Helping you to measure your progress, helps you to reach your target dates.

Ask yourself these reflective questions:

When will you know if the goal is complete?

3 Attainable

To make your goals attainable you have to have the self-belief that you will achieve them. Thinking positively about how you will attain them is a starting point.

4 Realistic

Do you realistically know if you can work towards your goal? How do you know that you can work towards the goal?

5 Timely

When do you want to have your goal in place? Are your colleagues, children or parents depending on you to achieve the goal? If it is for you, what difference will it make to your professional and personal development?

Appendix 2

'Action Amanda' has produced a fantastic DVD relating to promoting children's physical development. This DVD is ideal to use within 'jump and pump sessions.' Amanda, also works closely with 'Change for Life'

http://www.amandasactionclub.co.uk/Shop/ To purchase the DVD

http://www.nhs.uk/change4life/Pages/change-for-life.aspx

Appendix 3

Quarterly Evaluation

Name of Course:

What was most useful about this course and how has this impacted on your practice?

(Include how the course may have linked to the early years curriculum)

Have you been able to share the course content with your colleagues?

If yes, what aspects

Have you been on any other training and/or working towards a qualification?

If yes, please state and include how this course may have complemented this?

State any training that you feel may be relevant in supporting you in your role in helping children to achieve their outcomes.

Having had time to reflect; state how this course has been relevant to your continuous personal and

professional development and if you would recommend this course to others.

Appendix 4

United Nations Convention on the Rights of the Child

http://www.unicef.org.uk/Documents/Publication-pdfs/UNCRC_summary.pdf

Appendix 5

Helen Sanderson has created an original document called the 'One Page Profile' concept. It is a way that the child, parent and early educator can comment about the child's care and learning on one page. Using a One Page Profile can help to personalise how you teach and connect with children.

http://www.helensandersonassociates.co.uk/reading-room/how/person-centred-thinking/one-page-profiles.aspx

Sue Atkins has devised a course on the 'One Page Profile' concept:

http://sueatkinsparentingcoach.com/

Appendix 6

Quality improvement principals from the National Children's Bureau – NCB. Very helpful to support your practice and to reflect on quality

http://www.ncb.org.uk/nqin/resources/quality-improvement-principles

Appendix 7

For further information on Dr. Jools Page, 'Professional Love' concept, please read "Working with Babies and Children: From Birth to Three," Jools Page, Cathy Nutbrown and Ann Clare.

Appendix 8

Useful books on promoting sensory development:

Play Foundations-Senses — Laura Henry and Jeanette Phillips-Green

Sensory Play (Play in the EYFS) — Sue Gascoyne

Treasure Baskets & Beyond: Realizing the Potential of Sensory-rich Play — Sue Gascoyne

5179193R00050

Printed in Great Britain
by Amazon.co.uk, Ltd.,
Marston Gate.